God's Love Collapses The Centuries All

Reflecting with Saint Thérèse of Lisieux

God's Love Collapses The Centuries All

Reflecting with Saint Thérèse of Lisieux

Prayer Poems and Art
Sister Selena, O.C.D.
Carmel of the Resurrection
Indianapolis, Indiana

For
Rosemary Crump, O.C.D.
who, with Saint Thérèse,
is LOVE
in the heart of the Church

With Gratitude

Thank you, Mary Ellen Reed, of Marian College, Indianapolis, Indiana, for guiding me (most p-a-t-i-e-n-t-l-y <u>and</u> with great humor) into the magical and mysterious world of computer graphic design. Without the generous sharing of your experience and wisdom, this 'adventure' would never have been possible.

Thank you, Clare Bosler, of Indianapolis, Indiana, for devoting yourself enthusiastically to the large task of critiquing the reflections contained within.

Thank you, sisters of my community, for prayerfully supporting this project through its gestation, labor, and finally, its birth.

REFLECTIONS CONTAINED WITHIN

[continued]

REFLECTIONS CONTAINED WITHIN

SAINT THERESE OF LISIEUX

January 2, 1873 - September 30, 1897

Thérèse Martin's mother was a maker of Alençon Point Lace. My mother, as a child, hackled (combed) flax fibers used in the making of Irish lace. It was this simple maternal parallelism which first invited me into a rich personal relationship with Saint Thérèse of Lisieux. Previous attempts at appreciating her autobiography, *Story of a Soul,* and/or her other works were always curtailed by an inability to move beyond the rhetoric and flowery language style of Thérèse's time, nineteenth century France. However, once accustomed to this writing style, I began to uncover an incredible saga of a pampered, precocious child metamorphosed by God into a spiritual mentor for millions.

Thérèse's parents, Louis and Zelie, converted earlier thwarted desires for religious life into establishing the love and worship of God as the substantive core of their family life. Thus, from infancy, Thérèse was formed in daily routines of religious piety within the context of a loving, nurturing family who valued the Gospel principles of inclusiveness of all of God's creation.

The security and lovingness experienced by Thérèse are echoed in her own words:

> "Just as the sun shines simultaneously on tall cedars and on each little flower as though it were alone on earth, so Our Lord is occupied particularly with each soul as though there were no other like it." (*Story*, p. 14)

The result of this early foundation of love empowered Thérèse to develop a very personal relationship with a God whom she found "tender, merciful and loving" in an era when French Catholicism was permeated by fear of God and rigorism. Thérèse found it easy to trust her own insights and experience of God:

> "It seems to me that if a little flower could speak, it would tell simply what God has done for it without trying to hide its blessings." (*Story*, p. 15)

She also did not find it too terribly necessary to differentiate between God and Jesus. Her eyes, from an early age, were focused totally on God and Jesus.

It was this deeply formed faith which enabled Thérèse to survive the early loss of her mother and the loss of her older sisters-surrogate mothers-to the Carmel of Lisieux which would be home to Therese the last nine and a half years of her life.

Thérèse developed the spiritual maturity to understand that God wants "both our sacrifices <u>and</u> our joys." God desires our all. Indeed, Thérèse chose to do all, give all, be all for God and God's love-the way of love, THE LITTLE WAY, which is "very straight, very short." Thérèse was convinced that anyone with simple humility, honesty, and willingness to admit one's powerlessness, could walk her "way in all confidence and love."

I find Thérèse Martin's challenge of the loving way, THE LITTLE WAY, a wonderfully rewarding way to journey with God, to God. I invite you to journey with us both as with God's love we collapse the centuries all....

GOD' LOVE COLLAPSES THE CENTURIES ALL

"Two stems so tightly joined together put me in mind immediately of the mysteries of our souls...."

General Correspondence,Vol. II, p. 748

Collapsing the centuries
  is what we're about
  my 'old' little sister Thérèse and I.
Becoming friends in Christ
  through her words and life/
  my words and life.
Sharing the ways of our times.
Our likes, dislikes, attitudes and beliefs.
We're sharing it all
  with a joy-filled friendship unfolding
  as we trust in our God,
  who with LOVE
    collapses the centuries all.

GOING WHEREVER GOD LEADS

"Jesus does not demand great actions from us but simply surrender and gratitude."

Story of a Soul, p. 188

Water winds wherever,
        creating place as it goes
                establishing its truth by its being.
I go wherever God leads
        creating place as I go
                establishing my truth by my being.

GOD'S HEARTBEAT IS HEARD

"...a huge lake gilded by the sun's last rays, its calm waters blending their azure tints with the fires of the setting sun... seemed to understand already the grandeur of God and the marvels of heaven."

Story of a Soul, p. 125

At every point,
      in every place
        throughout this whole earth
        where water meets land,
the heartbeat of God is heard.
      Methodically,
          consistently,
               never-endingly,
that heartbeat of hope and renewal pulsates.
And,
      in that knowledge,
      I feel renewed in this moment.

TO BE A PEBBLE

"...I was growing in love for God, I felt within my heart certain aspirations unknown until then and at times I had veritable transports of love."

Story of a Soul, p. 112

I want to be a pebble
     dropped into
     the pool of eternity.
To descend into the darkness
     of Mystery
     absorbing God.
Then to ascend
     surface
     rippling Godness everywhere
warmly and simply
but
ever
so
profoundly.

GENTLE EXPLOSION OF CHANGE

"All great truths of religion, the mysteries of eternity, plunged my soul into a state of joy not of this earth... . I wanted to love, to love Jesus with passion, giving Him a thousand proofs of my love...."

Story of a Soul, p. 102

Gentle explosion of change
     erupt into new.
Purple our actions.
Violet our ways.
Mold us and make us
     pure,
     clear
     and simple.
Source of our being— all beings
we follow....

BE LOVE— SMILE

"I felt charity enter into my soul, and the need to forget myself and to please others...."

Story of a Soul, p. 99

Whiteness is the resurrection story.
Clear porcelain tone of our Savior's skin
     void of its bruises
     free of its pain.
White translucent glow radiating from Christ Jesus
     emitting healing
     invoking forgiveness.
Translucent glow touching us today.
Find the porcelain in today
     in the dark
     in the violent.
See the translucency in the powerless
     in the poor.
See the glow- God's glow
     in a smile.
Be the translucent
Be the glow
Be love.
Smile!

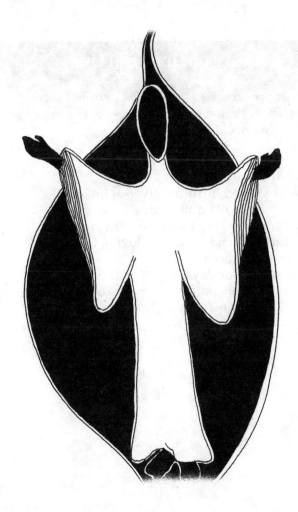

ENCIRCLE OTHERS IN LOVE

"...at the Last Supper, when Jesus knew the hearts of His disciples were burning with a more ardent love for Him who had just given Himself to them in the unspeakable mystery of His Eucharist, ... He said to them, that as I have loved you, you also love one another."

Story of a Soul, p. 219

Eucharistic wafer
    shaped in Your universal image,
      circle of endless love.
All our hopes begin with You, loving Alpha.
All our fears end with You, loving Omega.
Encircle our moments
Encompass our days.
Fill us with unending energy of Your love
    which may lovingly

ONION-LAYERED HEALING

"In spite of everything, I feel that I am filled with courage; I am sure that God is not going to abandon me."

General Correspondence Vol. I, p. 289

'Onion peeling' pain
     so tiring
     but so necessary
     to grow closer to You, O God.
To feel more of the warmth of Your love
     so many layers need shedding —
     layered years of living
        years of yearning.
The tons of 'onion peeling' tears produced
serve to baptize one ever more wholly
     into new realms of intimacy with You.
O God who created onions
     and onion-layered healing,
I thank You and praise You.

YOUR GRACE FIRST TOUCHED ME

"It was December 25, 1886, that I received...the grace of my complete conversion."

Story of a Soul, p. 98

My God, how did your grace first touch me?
     Suddenly,
     powerfully,
     yet, paradoxically felt through a breeze
     on an airless humid day.
Gently You enfolded me in nameless love.
     Safely,
     silently
     You held me,
     opening me to the knowing of timeless love
     which embraces all in all time.
Kaleidoscopic knowledge transcending all sense.
Wisdom without words.
Wonder without fear.
Your love infused me in that moment
     when breeze broke airless, endless time
     ventilating my dormant soul....
Thank You, my God, for renewed life!

PRAISE THE ONE WHO TUMBLES DOWN RAIN

"I was gazing at the grey skies from which a fine rain was falling every now and then...."

Story of a Soul, p. 15

Nuggets of rain tumble into a puddle
      each percolating aftershock ripplings
          who
               soundlessly bounce into others
          who
               in turn peacefully collide
          while
               still others rebound splashlessly.
The rain stops.
And all the wavelets vanish into one.

As the puddle parts have lived out John's Gospel
may we too one day all be one community
          joyously sharing love
          reverently living out forgiveness
          prayerfully praising The One
               who tumbles down nuggets of rain.

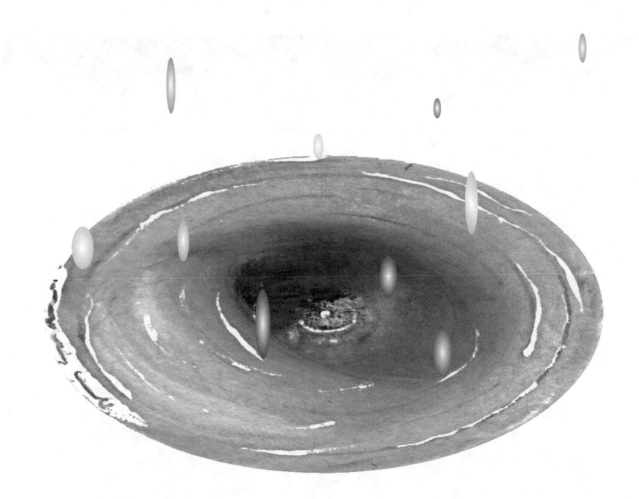

GOD'S LOVE— A HEALTHY ADDICTION

"...'draw me, we shall run'...suffices, I understand, Lord, that when a soul allows herself to be captivated... she cannot run alone, all the souls whom she loves follow in her train; this is done without constraint, without effort, it is a natural consequence of her attraction for You."

Story of a Soul, p. 254

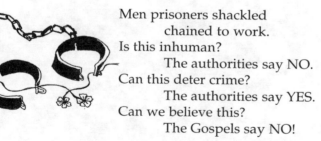

Men prisoners shackled
    chained to work.
Is this inhuman?
    The authorities say NO.
Can this deter crime?
    The authorities say YES.
Can we believe this?
    The Gospels say NO!

Women imprisoned
      denied even feminine protection.
Is this inhuman?
      The authorities say NO.
Can this deter crime?
      The authorities say YES.
Can you believe this?
      The Gospels say NO!

Addicted to loving God and others?
Can this be healthy?
      The Gospels say YES.
Can this be done?
      The Gospels say YES.
Do you believe it?
      Trust your YES!

THAT OTHER THREE-IN-ONE

"O my God! Most Blessed Trinity, I desire to love You and make You loved...."
Story of a Soul, p. 276

Did my presence startle you
      lithesome trio?
Don't fly off!
Yet,
      in your going, you give gift.
For as you ascend I'm invited to be awed by
      the expansiveness of your wings
      the agility with which you propel
         to such heights
      the beauty of your graceful
         winged patterns.
So silently
      so simply
         so elegantly
You move alone and still all three as one.

18

How you resemble that other Three-in-One
  whose expansiveness created all things in
  all time
  whose Word propelled people to new heights
    of consciousness
  whose Spirit silently, simply
    and yet so elegantly moves within us
    changing
    transforming
    invoking love.

WE'RE COSMICALLY BONDED

"... I am far from you, but it seems to me we are not separated. What does it matter where we are?"

General Correspondence Vol. I, p. 422

Not with hugs,
    loving warm embraces
    do I hold my loved ones.
Not close to me
    do they stay.
Yet we are connected,
    cosmically bonded
    in the trust of God's loving touch.

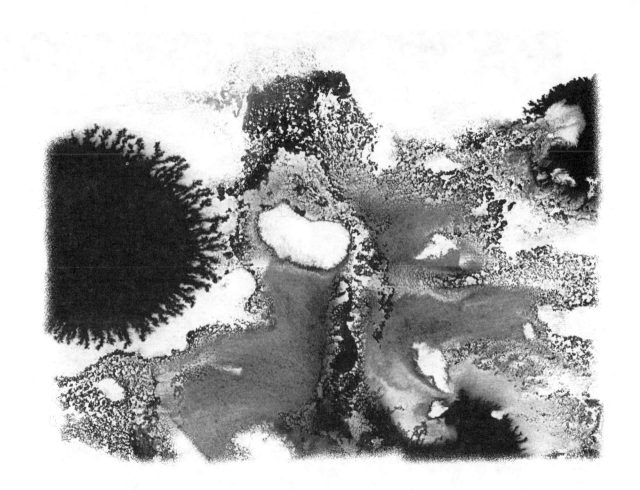

YOU ARE NOT ALONE

"Jesus, I do not know when my exile will be ended...."

Story of a Soul, p. 254

Atop a garden picked bouquet
     a tiny displaced ant frantically traverses its new terrain.
Lost in the vastness and newness of its surroundings
     the tiny ant wanders aimlessly.
Do ants know fear?
Do they experience the chill of uncertainty?
Will this exiled one be missed?

Atop the surface of this earthly sphere
     legions of our sisters and brothers
     wend their terrains of displacement.
Lost in the vastness of economic upheaval or political unrest
     these ants of humanity are forced to wander.
Do political peregrinators know fear?
Do these emigrants of economy experience the chill of uncertainty?
Are these exiled millions missed?

Atop my bed, I humbly pray for my nomadic siblings.
Please God, transform my prayerful petitions into
      work for a homeless one,
      food for a refugee family,
      loving adult protectors for an orphaned child.
Holy Spirit,creatively touch the heart of every itinerant, giving:
      courage to dispel fear,
      faith to dissolve uncertainty,
      forgiveness to combat bitterness.
Please,my exiled sisters and brothers,know
      YOU ARE NOT ALONE.
Each of you is carried most lovingly in this prayer....

BROTHER JESUS' LOVING RESPONSE

"I have noticed in all the serious circumstances of my life that nature always reflected the image of my soul."

Story of a Soul, p. 110

Causeway water rough and fierce is
      complementing my heart's uncertainty.
Leave or stay?
Fidelity to societal norms scream out STAY!
While God's will, I believe, signals LEAVE!
So again, this perplexed pilgrim travels to Saint Anne's Shrine,
      seeking her crucified grandson's guidance.

In bronze form, by water's edge,
My Brother Jesus hangs.
His face affirms my inner pain.
His heart avows my churning doubts.
Yet, I sense no relief in being with Him.
Should I stay? Should I leave?
No answer given,
      only the rough, fierce water echoes my inner tumult.

Days later
　　more confused, much more disconcerted
I return.
"Jesus Brother, please help me know!"
My Brother shares no response.
Dejected, downcast I open my eyes
　　and looking beyond my Brother's form
The waterline—
　　waveless, ripple-free, calm!
The prayer has answer.
The heart has calm.
I sense the ripplelessness of inner peace.

I left the Shrine.
I drove across the Causeway leaving an old life for a new.
And now,
　　whenever inner ripples rise,
　　if ever I sense doubt
I recall my Brother's loving response in calming
　　Lake Champlain.

SILHOUETTE MOMENT

"And still peace, always peace, reigned at the bottom of the chalice."

Story of a Soul, p. 167

Silhouette moment
    that particular time at end of day
    or start of new one
    when all is contoured into oneness.
Trees blend with bushes,
    bushes with grasses.
Birds against the sky's darkened background
    share winged resemblance.

If only we peoples could share silhouette moments
    of harmony and peace.
If only we could collectively come to trust in Our Creator of All
    at start of day to its end.
If only we would believe in The Light in our darkness.
If only....

27

A BARBER-OF-BUSHES

"When late in the year, the chestnut trees were pruned...."

The Last Conversations, p. 197

As a keeper-of-the-yard,
      a barber-of-the-bushes,
I find myself confounded.
How do I live peaceably with my brothers and sisters in nature
      as I yank weedlings,
      tear vines from their siblings,
      lop limbs off trees?

"Do I hurt you?" I asked
      as I thinned a lilac grove,
      patiently fleecing and slicing,
      cautiously clipping and pruning.
"Was that painful?" I inquired
      at completion of my morning's task.

A laugh broke the silence.
Abruptly turning,
I faced a matronly lilac who assured me I'd caused no harm.
"Quite the contrary, my dear,
      I think you've helped me feel at least fifteen years younger!"

FRANGIBLE THREAD OF GODNESS

"I understand now that I was making mental prayer without knowing it and that God was already instructing me in secret."

Story of a Soul, p. 75

Frangible thread of Godness
    unravels backwards.
From morning prayer
    to childhood memory.
Frightened child
    hiding in cellar's corner
    avoiding adult malevolence.
And,
    while in this 'secret space'
God came
    and held her fragile psyche
    in gentle blanketedness of prayer
    renewing/refreshing
    uplifting
        and refilling
    cloaking God's child
    in a fabric of invisible hopeful love.

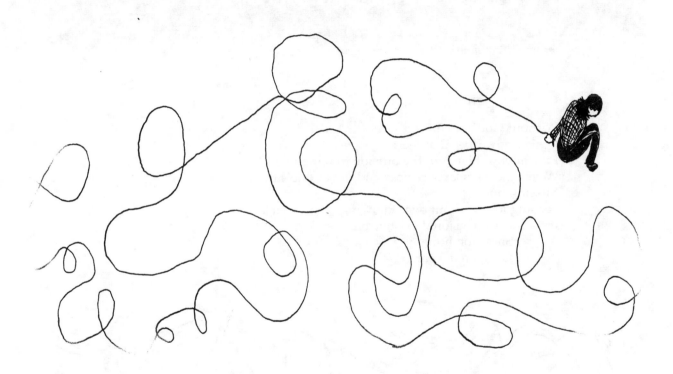

ROOTED IN THE FAITH OF GOD'S LOVE

"What a grace it is to have faith! If I had no faith, I would have inflicted death on myself without hesitating a moment."

Story of a Soul, p. 264

Without God's love,
      how does that feel?
Like always being on the outside looking in.
Wearing others' experiences and never one's own.
Missing out.
Sensing loss without ever knowing what is lacking.
It's a one dimensional existence.
      Short on hope
      Long on despair.

And, if that despair grows too consuming,
     if each day is carried more hopelessly,
     then one seeks release.
And when release forms stop numbing,
     one gives up.
Quits.
Dies.
Leaving others to ask, WHY?
Yet, didn't Jesus question despairingly,
     "My God, why have you forsaken me?"

But Jesus could move beyond his sense of devastation
     for He was rooted in the faith of God's love.
If one lacks that Knowledge-of-Rootedness
     ONE CAN'T MOVE.
One is simply swallowed into a dark futile abyss.

Knowing God's love is truly pure gift,
     a gift for which I daily give thanks
       to The One In Whom I find faith in my rootedness.

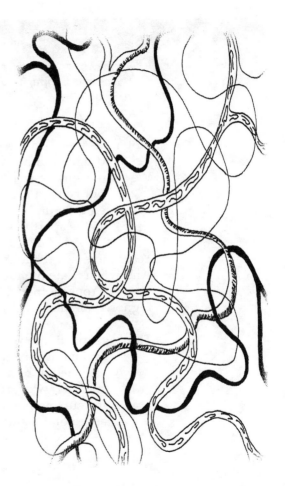

AN ADULT CHILD'S CONVERSION

"...I was able to pray at Mamma's grave and ask her to protect me always."

Story of a Soul, p. 73

Not a greeting card message relationship
     did my mother and I enjoy.
We shared surface space of house
     but none of heart at all.
I doubted even umbilical cord-ed-ness
     as the apartness felt so acute.

Years increased disunity but distance slowed the clash.
And when a late night call beckoned:
     "Your mother's ill— come quick!"
I ignored all filial feelings in responding to the call.

The days rolled into weeks, weeks flowed into months
     and months turned into years
     as I tried to be a daughter,
     such an awkward role to play
     for nursing home applications
     asked only name of next-of-kin not that of wounded child.

I begged my God to help me
      wear kindness and warm caring
      as days rolled into weeks,
          weeks flowed into months
              and months turned into years.

But not until her death time
      in the coldness of a winter
      in the bleakness of an ice storm
      that God in loving mercy transformed
      the coldness of my heart by freeing
      deep pained layered years.

Yes, in that ONE GRACED MOMENT
God immersed me in forgiveness,
      the kind that doesn't ever fade
      as my days roll into weeks,
          weeks flow into months
              and months turn into years....

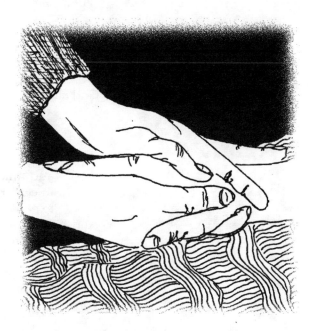

GOD SHOVELS MIST IN MORNING

"All my hope is in God alone."

Story of a Soul, p. 139

God shovels mist in morning
 at the start of brand new day
 guiding my morning thoughts
 into misted mood of prayer
 where richness flows
 and time converge
 in centered space without a place
 expansive without end.
And from this space I may
 explore the infinite of God
 to seek and find
 and taste and see
 beyond these words I speak.

All of it and then yet more
        infuse me with such love
        which flows to each and every heart
        of everyone on earth.
I feel the pain.
I know the throb of daily desolation.
I'm one with all the lost and poor,
        the homeless touch my heart.
I sense in God-filled oneness
        the power we call HOPE
        that shovel which God uses
        to tend the morning mist.

WHO WILL MEND GOD'S CHALICE ?

"Yes, I have found my place in the Church and it is You, O My God, who have given me this place; in the heart of the Church, I shall be LOVE."

Story of a Soul, p. 194

Who will mend the chalice
      God's Church throughout the world?
This vessel of tradition no longer accepted
      as exemplar for all.

The Truth is leaking out
      from chinks in chalice walls
      oozing into current hearts
      that message WE ARE ONE
      ordained to drink of one same Spirit
      the wellspring for us all.

Fear, the Church cement too long applied
        to block equality's egress
        is being dissolved, evaporated
        by those whose unscaled eyes
        can see beyond God's tarnished goblet
        to the essence of all Truth
        to live the Gospel message
        is to love without exception
        to love as Jesus loved-inclusively-
regardless of tradition.

So who will mend the chalice
        God's Church throughout our world?
Quite simply,
        who is God's loving glue?

HER GIGGLING LITTLE GUY

"What would become of me (in my suffering) if God did not give me courage? A person does not know what this is unless [s]he experiences it. No it has to be experienced."

Story of a Soul, p. 264

Her little son
     a giggling little guy
     is photographed in color
     at two among God's flowers.

When he was still a baby
     and their future seemed so full
     a doctor's diagnosis confirmed cancer in her body -
     catapulting all of them into a different realm where
     each moment really matters
     each incident and everyone is valued as pure gift.

She grew in true acceptance
     of the limitedness of her time
     bearing her cross courageously with humor and goodwill.
We cannot know all she endured as disease destroyed her body.
     but I cannot help think
     that in her bleakest moments, despair and difficult pain

that God's presence was shown in the daily little antics
of her son now photographed
at two among God's flowers.
For as flowers in their innocence
just by their simple being
give joy to joyless heart
and hope to desperate soul
then just imagine how much more
God gave in the joy-felt energy
of a TODDLER ON THE MOVE!

And so her God-given flower
a giggling little guy
brought hope and consolation
as she fought to hold each moment
as her spirit held to life.

But as she slept one evening
God gently lifted her to resurrected glory.
To each whose life she touched
she bequested a joyful zest for living
a legacy of love
most readily remembered in a photograph
of her giggling little guy
at two among God's flowers.

Her Son
(In memory of
Maureen Gagel Noland
8/26/64 - 7/31/95)

1995
1964
_____
31 years

LANGUAGE OF FAITH

"...you understand the language of faith better than that of the world..."

General Correspondence, Vol.II, p. 865

Languedoc, in the south of France means
    'The Land of the language of Yes'.
Imagine such a vision
      truly a blessed dream
        a place where God's stamp of YES is imprinted
          on each and all.

There'd be no violence, hate or crime
      and children could live hopeful,
        not permeated with fear.
Their lives would model oldsters
      compassionate and loving
It's a place where even in times of darkness
      faithfulness would carry the-heart-of-heavy-times.

For Jesus in YES language
        assuringly reminds us
        'I will never leave you.
                I love you more than life'.
In His words, all can sense
        the joy of resurrection
        the lastingness and lovingness
                which infiltrates the attitudes
                contaminates all actions
        of ones who see beyond the NO of overt reality
        to YES of Truth's sublimity,
                redemptive actuality,
         God's never- ending love.

SIMPLICITY IN LIFE

"I love simplicity; I have a horror for pretense."

Last Conversations, p. 77

Does one have to live a monk's life
of silence, fast and prayer
to tap into the motherload of simplicity
in this life?

Can one be worldly busy
wear its pressures as a skin
and still keep God's priority,
authentic love
as maxim for one's life?

To reach into one's center
      and uncover what is Real.
To separate extraneous from
      richness in God's Truth.
To dare to challenge convention
To doubt the mainstream's thought.
To pick and choose,
      finding strength in choices made
To pattern joy to others
      whether same-thinking or not.
To stretch in understanding
      to grow with faithfulness.
To laugh and cheer and celebrate
      God's loving gift for all,
      which is most succinctly

SIMPLICITY IN LIFE!

SISTER SOLITUDE

"... the gifts which God showered upon me drew me to Him; and I saw that He alone was unchangeable, that He alone could fulfill my immense desires."

Story of a Soul, p. 175

Sister solitude
Waltz me into the never-endingness of newness
Of the tempo set by God
      quiet
            pause
                  quiet
                        pause.

Motion of millenniums
movement of my soul.
I dance with you amid the din
I glide with you in restful place.
Sister of my solitude
      remain my inner friend.

HOLY MOTHER'S TENDER SMILE

"It seems to me the Blessed Virgin must have looked upon her little flower and smiled at her, for wasn't it she who cured her with a visible smile?"

Story of a Soul, p. 78

To same chapel I daily went to pray.
A painting of the Crucified One
  long held my eyes' attention.
But one morning I found it replaced
  by an iconized life-size Mother and Her Infant Son.
I found the change disturbing
  though I could not reason why.
And daily eye-dueling did ensure.
She stared at me— I stared at she.
Why was this act upsetting?

Then one morning I felt a tear
  my heart began to ache
  old memories and yesterdays
   vividly replaying.
I looked at this other Mother
  whose eyes were fixed on me
   and felt a deepening bondedness
   my anguish she could feel.
I sensed a real compassion— her commiseration great.

Thus to same chapel I continued to daily go.
The inner wounds were touched, examined,
        sutured,
under the gentle gaze of Our Loving Holy Mother.
She knew my heart,
        I trusted her.
So it was not surprising
        when looking up one morning
I found in her expression—
                a genuine, loving smile!

I sensed with time the pain would end,
        the sutures they'd dissolve.
She gave my heart a new-felt joy,
        my soul a hope-filled light,
and still today when I seek help
        I can recall
Our Holy Mother's gentleness in her tender loving smile!

BABY QUILTS

"Little children are not damned."

Last Conversations, p. 84

Baby quilt cozy and warm
Stitched by love
           concern
           care.
Baby quilt frayed and tattered
Stitched by neglect
           abuse
           oppression.

O, One-All-Merciful,
Unconditional Love,
           who creates all patterns
           equalize the stitchings please.
Give the insights
Teach the wisdom
        so we may learn
           how ALL Your children
        may receive preferential treatment.

THE LOVING FLOW OF GOD

"I offer myself a victim of holocaust to your merciful love...allowing the waves of infinite tenderness shut up within You to overflow into my soul and that I may become a martyr of your love, O my God."

The Story of a Soul, p. 277

Deep in the core of a simple calla lily
     I encountered the omnipresence of God.
Eyes drawn first to the stately, simplistic contour
     which flows into itself
          encircling itself
     inviting one ever so gently into
          its mysterious center
     where one's eyes strain to peer into
          its ever widening depth
               which opens into seeming vortical motion
     transcendentally captivating,
          mesmerizing
               leaving one sensing the loving flow of God.

GATHERING OF WOMEN

"Ah poor women, how they are misunderstood! And yet they love God in much larger numbers than men do and during the Passion of Our Lord, women had more courage than the apostles since they braved the insults of the soldiers and dared to dry the adorable Face of Jesus. It is undoubtedly because of this that He allows misunderstanding to be their lot on earth, since He chose it for Himself. In heaven, He will show that His thoughts are not men's thoughts, for then the last will be first."

Story of a Soul, p. 140

Garlands of corn rows
  glow in the sunshine
Woven together by fields
  of wild clover.
Yellows and white
  sprinklings of purple.
Crown of God's glory
  simple and pure.

Gathering of women
  glow in God's sunshine
Woven together in spirit
  of wisdom.
Young ones and olders
  with sprinkling of gray
Crown of God's glory
  simple and pure.

MOUNTAIN OF ETERNITY

"Oh! How sweet is the way of love! How I want to apply myself to doing the will of God always with the greatest of self surrender!"

Story of a Soul, p. 181

Mountain of eternity
O God, you are our awesome pinnacle.
    Into the depths one journeys
        guided only by fathomless longing
    to silently climb Your heights.
Ascending by descending
    into the darkness of Your Light
        the Light which offers
            hope and possibility
        in the midst of our fractured contemporary times.
The Light which invites us to love
    and be loved
        by the mystery of You,
    O Mountain of Eternity.

OUR ALTERED MOMENTS

"When God stretches out His hand to ask, His hand is never empty, and thus intimate friends can draw from Him the courage and strength they need."

Story of a Soul, p. 110

For whom the nearby sirens scream,
    I pray.
For those in need of assistance,
    for those rendering aid.
To each give courage, compassion
    and faith.
Faith to believe whatever the circumstances
    there be a solution.
Faith which provides real hope
    especially in times of disaster or distress.

How quickly our moments can be altered.
What is reality now
    can in a blinking, be forever changed.
O God, whose love is never-changing,
    please give reminders of Your love
        to each affected by
            nearby screaming sirens.

SEASONS OF FORGIVENESS

"He wants me to love Him because He has forgiven me not much but ALL!"

Story of a Soul, p. 84

In pure cyclic process
    flow the seasons of forgiveness
    as those of nature's time.
The darkness of a winter
    with underlying growth
    which blossoms forth in springtime
    unburdening the heavy heart.
The sunshine of God's lovingness
    brings a summer of new hope
    with scales of soul-crustedness falling
    as do the autumn leaves.
As mysterious as nature's time
    are the seasons of forgiveness
    which unfold whenever
    a simple invocation of willingness
    is given to our ever-present God.

UNMERITED LOVE

"I cannot conceive a greater immensity of love than the one which it has pleased You to give me freely, without any merit on my part."

Story of a Soul, p. 256

Unmerited love reveals itself
    in a plethora of ways.
That cloudy drizzly day
    breaking summer's squeltering heat,
    the kindness extended when not expected.
Verbal encouragement.
Non-verbal caring.
A humorous tale told
    de-clogging the mind of "serious stuff."

God-Of-All-Giving,
    thank You
   for revealing Yourself
    in a plethora of wonderful ways
      in the moments of my days.

SHADOW SUIT

"One would have to travel through this dark tunnel to understand the darkness."

Story of a Soul, p. 212

Shadow suit.
We all own one.
Fear, insecurity
      sends one into the closet of darkness
      to drag it out.
Crawl into it.
It fits comfortably.
It feels safe.
But only when worn
      for a time that its heaviness is felt—
      suffocating
      smothering
      somehow stifling all else.
God alone can help remove it.
Gently eases one out from under its weight.
"I want to get rid of it," I scream, when freed from its burden.
"O no" gently coaxes my God.
"Smile at it. Accept it. You own it,
      yet,
      you need not wear it, this shadow suit of yours.
But, love it—it's you!"

PEACE WAS A STRANGER TODAY

"God answered the prayer He inspired me to direct to Him in favor of one of His suffering members."

Story of a Soul, p. 38

Sanctuary lamp's
    pale blue glow
        in darkened chapel
            gently comfort
                as all for whom
                    peace was a stranger today
                        are lovingly cradled in humble
                            prayer.

GIVER OF JOY — THANK YOU

"It is with great happiness, then, that I come to sing the mercies of the Lord...."

Story of a Soul, p. 15

Squirrel tail tangled in fallen leaf
    recalls apple picking times.
Plucking the ripe ones
    finding the 'dropsies'—
    a delight in adventuring.

Anticipating with glee
    apple cinnamon aromas—
    tarts, pies, and cobblers.
Sweet smells of a season
    simple and crisp.

God in the redness, the yellow, the green.
God of such goodness,
    giver of joy.
Thank You for apples, Autumn and You.

ANGELUS BELLS PEALING

"...it seems to me that Love penetrates and surrounds me, at each moment this Merciful Love renews me."

Story of a Soul, p. 181

Archetypal action of ten centuries
      the Angelus bells pealing
            praise to our Mother of God.
Cosmic cord
      tolling forth energy of our nurturing parent—
Comforter,
      one who modeled love for her son,
           the One Chosen.

Chime again
      reverberations of God's soothing love.
Angelus Domini—
God's angel bring anew—ring anew
      the message of hope and healing
      to our aching hearts,
      our needy souls—
      our very wounded world.

OCTOBER'S VIOLET

"For me, prayer is an aspiration of the heart, it is a simple glance directed to heaven. It is a cry of gratitude and love in the midst of trial as well as joy; finally it is something great, supernatural, which expands my soul and unites me to God."

Story of a Soul, p. 242

October's violet
     houses the infinite of the I AM
         and the perception of my I AM
     within the framework of all eternity.

In its tiny core
     merge that message of union
     God in me/I in God.
Oneness
Mystery
Peace within the purple folds of October's violet.

JESUS, WHO ARE YOU?

"I made the resolution never to wander far away from the glance of Jesus in order to travel peacefully towards the eternal shore."

Story of a Soul, p. 49

Jesus,
   Who are you, where are you?
    I'm spiritually shambled
       in need of a picture to put focus
       back on You.

    I'm in the face of your family,
       the feelings of friends.
    I'm found in the helpless,
       the indigent,
       the lost.

    I'm laughter in children
       as giggling girls
       or the chucklings of boys.
   I'm surrogate mother,
       long- lost brother.

I'm counselor
    hand holder
    hug giver
    night lover if that's what is needed.

I'm hope in the sunrise
    faith in day's dusk.
I'm chirp of the small bird,
    wag of dog's tail.

I'm in all
    and with all
    to all who believe.
So listen in quiet
    and you'll quickly find
    the picture you'll need
    dear portraitist of mine.

O MAGICIAN OF TRANSFORMATION

"I didn't have enough... to rise above these miseries of life, so my poor little heart suffered very much."

Story of a Soul, p. 53

What to do about Eli
     prayingly beseeched a woman
     referring to a boy,
          a mere child she called him,
     who set fire to her garage.
The concern was not for the garage
     nor the fire set within.
She cares about Eli
     the latch-key child
     the lonely child.
The lost child being raised by a single parent
     just a child herself.

Eli, Eli,— My God, My God
    please don't abandon Your little namesake.
In Your wondrous way
        O Magician of Transformation
            sprinkle hope into Eli's heart
            and the millions of other children
            who deserve a conjured cure
                for growth
                        and life
                            and grace.

AS SEASONS MOVE ALONG

"There are things the heart feels but which the tongue and even the mind cannot express."

Story of a Soul, p. 37

Gentle light of late Autumn morn
rests on the leaf-bear tree
keeping warm the now naked limbs
as seasons move along.

As seasons move along
we too, in nakedness,
are held gently in the Light of The One
whose birth season we soon anticipate
which warms our HOPE
for PEACE and LOVE
in this our turbulent world.

BEING WOMBED IN GOD

"Never will I forget the impression the sea made upon me...everything spoke to my soul of God's grandeur and power."

Story of a Soul, p. 48

Marie, at seventy
    birthed a dream
    conceived at six while
    cloistered on a rural farm.
This dream,
    [lain dormant
        in later years as Marie lived
           cloistered yet again,
              behind a convent wall]
    was
to stand ankle deep in ocean suds
    and feel its spray baptizing her
    into God's flowing ageless grace.

Being one with all oceans
      all seas
all that wombs us and warms us
all that calls us to the One
      who creates us new in each moment.
To harmonize with waves' timeless tunes
      and dance with sandpipers
      and grandchildren of the ancient gulls
while being absorbed into infinity
      beyond distant horizon gaze.
To smell the salted scent of history's long
          recorded time
and touch its precious shelled keepsakes
created before all history's time.
Just to be at the ocean!

Again Marie is cloistered
      behind Alzheimer's walls
but, nonetheless,
      I believe
Marie continues to recount
      the day she birthed
      that long-held dream
      of being wombed in God.

FIELDS OF CLOUDS

"We have, then, only to surrender our soul, to abandon it to our great God...."

General Correspondence Vol. II, p. 861

Fields of clouds
  hide me away for just briefly,
  as do cornfields children at play.
Pocket me.
Hold me.
Perhaps let me peek between your patches of eternity.

Just for a moment or few
    I need to move away from our seemingly difficult,
        heavy world—
    violence clones violence
    disease devastates
    injustice runs amok.

                O One-Who-Creates-All-Cloud-Fields
                  renew my faith.
                  Restore me.
                Let me feel as free as children at play.

LOVING PROVIDER OF PINE CONES

"I felt it was far more valuable to speak to God than to speak about God...."

Story of a Soul, p. 87

To begin anew in this moment
to turn again to You
who ingeniously created the evergreens
diluting the starkness of winter's transitional nakedness,
making evident Your Mystery.

How obvious Your omniscience
in the symmetrical configurations of pine needle families.
Separate
yet melded harmoniously
as is Your desire for all creation
unity
harmony
mutuality
all communally striving to live out Your message of universal love.

May Your will be done,
      Loving Provider of Pine Cones and all....

NIGHT STAR OF YOUR BIRTH SKY

"O Jesus...I beg You to cast Your Divine Glance upon a great number of little souls...worthy of Your Love."

Story of a Soul, p. 2

Baby Jesus blanketed in night
    this night
    night of your birth
    night holding a glistening star
    before whose birth You originate.
Star, which, if eyes strain,
    appears as a cross—
    as the cross from which You will hang
    in giving ALL for us.

Night star of Your birth sky
    bedazzling jewel
    bemoaning destiny
    may it innocently delight You Baby Jesus
    while Your Coming enraptures afresh
Your loving hope of redemption
    joy of resurrection
As Your eternal glance fixes on us all.

PROMISE PIERCES

"I felt that the only thing necessary was to unite myself more and more to Jesus and that 'all these things will be given besides'."

Story of a Soul, p. 238

A soldier pierced one man's side
　　　and the transforming unitive vision of Jesusian Hope
　　　penetrated into the deep of cosmic consciousness
　　　forever changing our world.

Again tonight
　　　Easter Vigil darkness is broken by the Light of Jesus Christ
　　　resurrecting God's glory
Piercing promise into our world.

Energy of love
        aura of warm
        protect
        project
        pierce promisingly into all
        who endeavor to do Your will
                to love Your love
                to shine Your light.

Piercing Promise
        hold those who can't feelYou
                        see You
                        sense You.

        Carry and support
        nurture and sustain
Christ Jesus our Promise
        pierce ever more deeply into our darkness.

FIAT OF THIS MOMENT

"Everything is grace."

Story of a Soul, p. 266

There's a freedom in forgiveness
    which comes by God-given-grace.
There's a joy in opening self
    to the nudging of God's touch.
There's a peacefulness
    when choosing the 'fiat' of the moment.
There's a wonderment in knowing
    that the unknowingness of All
    is capsulated within each of all on earth.
And,
    it's sacramental Mystery
    which stirs the heart anew
    on each occasion when God's love
    IS revealed in a microcosmic way....